Step By Step Along the

APPALACHIAN TRAIL

Step By Step Along the
APPALACHIAN TRAIL

Latch door when leaving
or porcupines will eat
this building.

Tricia
Andryszewski

Twenty-First Century Books
Brookfield, Connecticut

Cover photographs courtesy of David Muench Photography
(top © David Muench), © Jerry & Marcy Monkman/EcoPhotography
(2nd from top), © Joe & Monica Cook (left, bottom),
Great Smoky Mountains National Park (right)

Photographs courtesy of © Joe & Monica Cook: pp. 3 (left, center left), 5
(center), 16, 19, 23, 26, 37, 47, 50, 51; David Muench Photography, Inc.:
pp. 3 (right center © Marc Muench; right © David Muench), 5 (left © Marc
Muench), 13 (© David Muench), 21 (© David Muench), 27 (© Marc
Muench), 38 (© Marc Muench), 40 (© David Muench), 42 (© David
Muench), 58 (© David Muench), 61 (© David Muench); © Jerry &
Marcy Monkman/EcoPhotography: pp. 5 (right), 54; The Portland
(Maine) Newspapers: p. 8; Great Smoky Mountains National Park: p. 20;
Appalachian Trail Conference: p. 29 (Nick Williams); Visuals Unlimited:
p. 33 (© Mark E. Gibson); Appalachian Mountain Club: p. 59 (Al Falcione)

Library of Congress Cataloging-in-Publication Data
Andryszewski, Tricia, 1956–
Step by step along the Appalachian Trail / Tricia Andryszewski.
p.   cm.
Summary: An overview of the natural history of the Appalachian Trail
and of historical events related to the route, an imaginary hike up the trail,
and a description of what can be seen and experienced along the way.
ISBN 0–7613–0273–5 (lib. bdg.)
1. Hiking—Appalachian Trail—Juvenile literature.   2. Nature study—
Appalachian Trail—Juvenile literature.   [1. Hiking. 2. Nature study.
3. Appalachian Trail.]   I. Title.
GV199.42.A68A53   1998
796.51'0974—dc21   98–7304   CIP   AC

Published by Twenty-First Century Books
A Division of The Millbrook Press, Inc.
2 Old New Milford Road
Brookfield, Connecticut 06804

CONTENTS

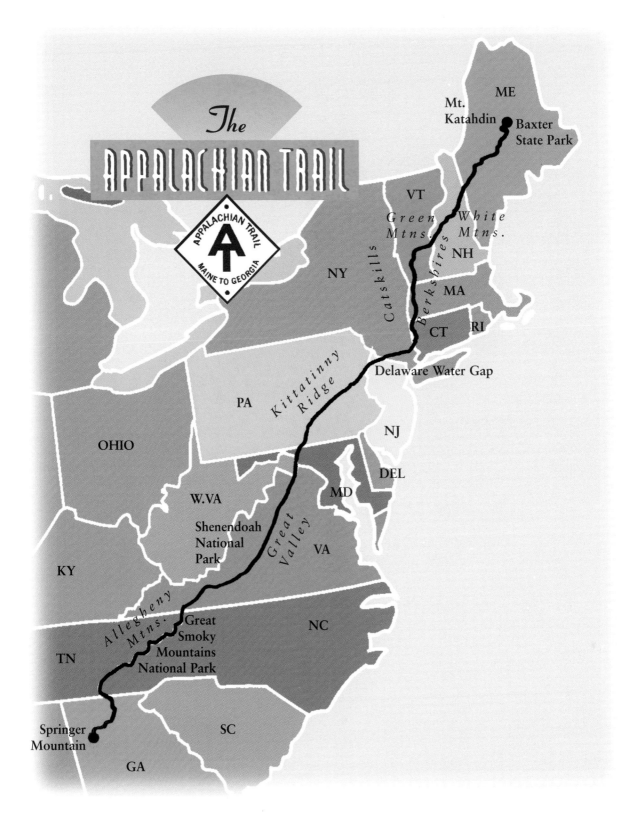

The Big PICTURE

APPALACHIAN TRAIL
GEORGIA TO MAINE
A Footpath for Those who Seek
Fellowship with the Wilderness
(sign atop Springer Mountain, Georgia)

The Appalachian Trail runs for more than 2,150 miles (3,460 kilometers), from Georgia to Maine, along the ridges of the Appalachian mountain ranges. These mountains are hundreds of millions of years old—older than the Rocky Mountains, older than Mount Everest in the Himalayas.

Earthquakes and Glaciers

Our planet is nearly four and one-half billion years old. Over these billions of years, the place on the earth's surface that we now call the United States has been shaped and reshaped many times. Huge pieces of the earth's crust have slowly moved and mashed together, crumpling up

Building a mountain range

The AT traces the ridge of the oldest mountain range in North America. Here's how scientists believe the Appalachians were formed.

1 440 million years ago

Earth's drifting continents begin to collide.

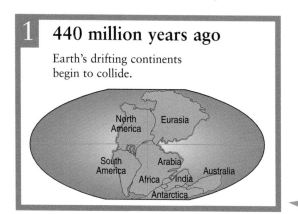

2 410–360 million years ago

Collision folds eastern edge of North America. Appalachians are born.

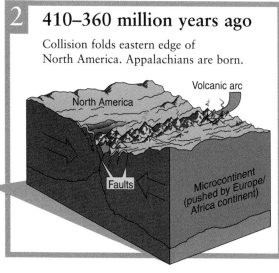

3 360–245 million years ago

Continental collision ends. Young Appalachians are as tall as present-day Andes or Rockies.

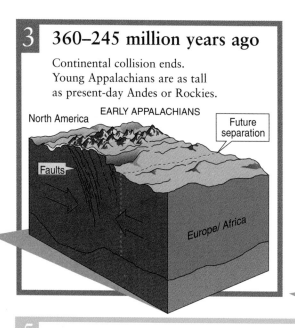

4 245 million years ago to present

Atlantic Ocean opens. Appalachians erode.

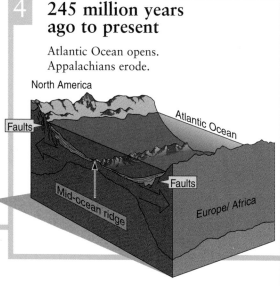

5

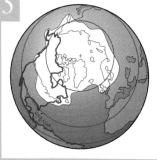

Starting about 1.5 million years ago, a series of great glaciers advance southward from the arctic and reshape the northern Appalachians. When the glaciers recede—most recently between 13,000 and 11,000 years ago—they scour humps of bedrock, carve lakes, and dump vast deposits of rock, gravel, and clay.

into mountain ranges such as the Appalachians. The Earth's crust is still moving today, right under your feet. Most of the time, this movement is too slow and quiet to be seen or heard. Once in a while, though, it slips suddenly—in an earthquake.

The North American continent settled down into more or less the shape we see today only about sixty million years ago—about the time the dinosaurs died out. In the West two long lines of mountains rose up—first the Rocky Mountains and then the Pacific coast mountains.

Meanwhile, in the eastern half of North America, the much older Appalachian mountain ridges stood even taller and sharper than they look today. Over hundreds of millions of years, much of these mountains has been washed away by the rain and blown away by the wind. Bit by bit, rock and sand and soil have rolled down from the Appalachians. To the west of the Appalachians, the Great Plains have grown flatter and flatter, covered by layer after layer of stuff washed down from the mountains. On the other side of the Appalachian mountains, the eroded bits of mountain have spread out into a wide plain stretching east into the Atlantic Ocean.

About a million years ago, icy weather began to change the surface of the northern part of North America. For hundreds of years at a time during this ice age, summers didn't heat up enough to melt away all of the previous winters' snows. Layer after heavy layer of snow compacted into enormous packs of ice called glaciers. These glaciers spread out over the northern, colder part of the continent like pancake batter dropped on a griddle. At one time or another, ice hundreds or even thousands of feet thick covered all of New England, most of the Midwest, and many scattered spots in the western half of North America.

Toward the end of the ice age, the first people to settle in America walked across the bridge of land that then stretched from Asia to Alaska. These first Americans and their descendants spread out over North America, reaching the central and southern Appalachian mountains as early as 11,000 years ago.

The great glaciers never reached the southern half of the Appalachian mountain ranges. But the centuries of colder-than-normal weather changed even the southern-most Appalachian mountains. The cold killed many kinds of trees and other plants and animals, even south of where the glaciers grew.

The glaciers grew four times during the cold centuries of the ice age. (In between, the glaciers retreated, melting during hundreds of years of warmer weather.) They last retreated up toward the North Pole about 10,000 years ago. They may return someday.

The weight of all that glacial ice compacted the earth beneath it, pressing the landscape down by hundreds of feet. The surface sprang back, though not completely, once the ice was gone.

Farther north, the retreating glaciers left behind a bare, scraped-clean landscape without many plants and animals. In many places, much of the soil needed for plants to grow in had been scraped away as well, with nothing but rock left showing.

All that soil didn't just disappear. The moving ice had pushed it, along with a lot of rock, to the glaciers' edges, where it dropped out when the ice finally melted. The rich soil of the best New England farmland was left behind by melting glaciers. So were incredible numbers of rocks of all sizes. You can still see these rocks along the Appalachian Trail in New England today.

Even in places where soil was lost to the glaciers, rather than gained, enough scraps remained to support a few plants here and there. Year after year, the plants grew, died, rotted, and made compost for future generations of more and more plantlife. Eventually, over thousands of years, forests grew where the glaciers had been.

10

By a few thousand years ago, North America had pretty well bounced back from the effects of the glaciers. The climate by then was warmer, much like it is today. And the scenery was much like what it would be today if so many people had not come to live here—a thick cover of forest stretching from the ocean westward, over the Appalachian mountains to the grasslands of the Great Plains.

The Appalachian Mountains

The Appalachian mountains themselves are made up of many smaller groups of mountains, each of which has its own unique character.

Native Americans living here before the arrival of the first Europeans didn't much change the Appalachian landscape. In some places they did try to change the natural environment to meet their needs. Patches of forest were burned clear to improve farming and hunting, for example. But the Native Americans were few in number, and spread thinly over a lot of land. They didn't use up more of the Appalachian mountains' many natural resources than nature could replace.

The Settling of the Appalachians

This picture changed when people from Europe came to live in North America. At first, most of the newcomers settled close to the Atlantic Ocean. But in the 1700s and early 1800s, as millions upon millions more arrived, the flat, rich farmland near the Atlantic coast kept getting more and more crowded and expensive.

Hemmed in at first by the Appalachian mountains, people soon moved inland to less crowded land. The steeper land in the mountains was more difficult to farm, but it was also cheaper, and in time it too began to attract farmers and other settlers. As they settled the land running up into the Appalachian hills, they cleared away the forest to make farmland, using the trees for fuel and building materials. By the mid-1800s, most of America's great eastern forest—including the forest covering most of the Appalachian mountains—had been cut down and plowed up.

It's hard to farm well on a mountainside. Once the forest was cut down, rain soon washed the richness out of the soil on the Appalachian mountain slopes. Each year, hillside farmers from New England to Georgia got less food out of the crops grown on their washed-out, worn-out soil.

When the Great Plains began to open up to pioneer settlers toward the end of the 1800s, many of these Appalachian farmers left their worn-out farms behind and moved west. Trees grew up on many of the farms they left behind.

These new patches of forest were different from the original unbroken old-growth forest. Some of the animals that had been killed or forced out of the Appalachian mountains by the farmers never returned, or returned to only a small part of the areas where they used to live. But many forest animals made a big comeback—deer especially, but also bears, beavers, foxes, wild turkeys, and more.

The Appalachian Trail

By the early 1900s, the Appalachian mountain range was a patchwork quilt of worn-out farmland mixed with patches of scruffy new woods and some older woods. The land-use planner Benton MacKaye looked out over this patchwork and saw a wonderful possibility: Why not have a long wilderness footpath through these mountains? It would be close enough to the big Eastern cities to give the city dwellers a chance to hike in the woods. "America needs her forests and her wild spaces quite as much as her cities and her settled places," he wrote.

An article by MacKaye, published in 1921, urged that the Appalachian Trail be created and preserved. Groups of nature lovers set to work on the Trail right away. From the beginning, as much of the Trail as possible was located in public parks and public forests. The first section of the Trail was completed in 1923, in Harriman State Park (now Bear Mountain State Park), in New York. The last section of the Trail was blazed in 1937, in Maine.

The Georgia Appalachian Trail Club had this plaque made to mark the beginning of "A Footpath for Those who seek Fellowship with the Wilderness."

Blind thru-hiker Bill Irwin and his dog guide, Orient, took eight months to complete the Trail, from early March to early November 1990. "Going downhill was the most difficult and dangerous part," he later wrote. "Uphill was hard on my back, legs and lungs, but no one ever got killed falling uphill. . . . Every time I went down, I tried to be thankful I wasn't hurt worse than I was."

Irwin fell thousands of times, pack and all, during his thru-hike. His worst injury was a cracked rib.

In 1968, Congress passed the National Scenic Trails Act. This law named both the Appalachian Trail in the East and the Pacific Crest Trail in the West as "National Scenic Trails." (Since then, several other National Scenic Trails have been named.) The act also promised that the U.S. government would define and protect a zone of wilderness all along the Appalachian Trail.

Sections of the Trail are relocated from time to time, so the Trail can follow the best and most wild and scenic route possible. There are still some bits of the Trail that follow roads, although the trail managers try to avoid this. And not all of the Trail is on parkland. Some sections still pass through private land owned by people who have kindly agreed to allow hikers through.

The Thru-hikers

In 1948, Earl Shaffer became the first person to walk the full length of the Trail in one continuous trip. (Several hikers had already walked all of the Trail in sections, but no one had done it in one hike from end to end.) Along the way, Shaffer met people who thought he was crazy or who simply didn't believe him when he told them what he was doing. Even many of the Trail's creators doubted that such a feat was possible—but Shaffer did it anyway.

Since Shaffer, more than 3,000 people of all ages and backgrounds have thru-hiked the Trail (walked its full length), either in sections or in one continuous hike. Currently, about 1,200 to 1,500 hikers set out to thru-hike the Trail each year. Only about 200 succeed.

Georgia
North Carolina
AND TENNESSEE

The Appalachian Trail in Georgia, North Carolina, and Tennessee takes hikers through some of the roughest, wildest, toughest mountain hiking in the eastern United States. The trail here also runs the length of the Great Smoky Mountains National Park—America's most popular national park.

Springer Mountain to Fontana Lake

The Appalachian Trail begins on the top of Springer Mountain, in Georgia, and the climb up is long and steep. Plenty of would-be thru-hikers have decided to cancel their plans to hike the whole Appalachian Trail before reaching the top of the mountain. There, at 3,782 feet (1,153 meters) above sea level, is the southern end of the great footpath running high in the Appalachian mountains, over hundreds of mighty mountain peaks, from Georgia all the way to Maine.

15

Cherokee Indians living near where the Appalachian Trail now runs in the South were forced to leave their homes and move west after gold was discovered in the hills nearby. Thousands died along the "Trail of Tears" during the Cherokees' deadly winter trek to Oklahoma in 1838. Millions of dollars worth of gold was mined in their former homeland in the 1840s.

Thru-hikers heading north begin their long journey by signing the hikers' register kept on top of Springer Mountain. Only a few will make it to the Trail's northern end, on top of Mount Katahdin in Maine—four to six months, fourteen states, and more than 2,150 miles (3,460 kilometers) later.

Heading north from Springer Mountain, the Appalachian Trail rollercoasters up and down forested hills through the Chattahoochee National Forest, heading for the Trail's highest peak in Georgia, Blood Mountain, 4,461 feet (1,360 meters) above sea level.

A sunset view from the top of Springer Mountain, Georgia.

Blood Mountain got its name from a terrible battle fought on and near the mountain by Cherokee Indians and Creek warriors who invaded their territory. Nearby Slaughter Mountain got its name from the same battle.

The trees are tall here, with lots of oak and other hardwoods—but this isn't virgin forest. In the 1800s, the trees were cut down on these mountainsides, and for a while the land became farmland. By the early 1900s, though, the farms were mostly worn out, the farmers mostly gone. The trees began to grow back, becoming the forest you see today.

At Bly Gap, 76 miles (122 kilometers) up the Trail from Springer Mountain, the Trail crosses over from Georgia into North Carolina. The state boundary is also the boundary between Chattahoochee National Forest and the Nantahala National Forest, which the Trail passes through for the next 59 miles (47 kilometers).

Hikers agree that the Trail through the Nantahala Mountains is steep, tough, and rugged. Just a few miles up the Trail from the state border, a short side trail leads to the top of Standing Indian Mountain, 5,498 feet (1,676 meters) high. A few miles up and down the hills later comes Wayah Bald—5,342 feet (1,628 meters) above sea level—and even tougher hiking lies ahead. Many thru-hikers have said that the steep hiking from where the Trail crosses the Nantahala River to where it reaches Fontana Lake is the most difficult section of the entire Appalachian Trail.

The Appalachian Trail meets the southern tip of Fontana Lake at Fontana Dam. At 480 feet in height from

Climate on the Trail
Springtime comes earlier in the warmer valleys, and works its way up to the colder Appalachian mountaintops. Mountain hikers can walk uphill from a valley's springtime warmth and greenness into an icy winter mountaintop landscape, then back down into spring again, all in a few hours. Spring also comes earlier in the South than in the North. Thru-hikers starting their long walk at the southern end of the Appalachian Trail walk north with the spring in April and May.

When Orient, the guide dog, "came to a complete stop one day on a narrow portion of the Trail, I thought we had met a hiker coming from the other direction. I said hello and wondered why the person didn't say anything in reply.

"I don't remember what I said next, . . . but Orient growled and I became aware that whatever was standing ahead of us was grinding its teeth. . . .

"When I realized that the thing on the Trail in front of me was a bear, I tried to explain that my food bag was almost empty and that I hadn't seen a candy bar in days. I mentioned that I was just passing through the area and promised not to pick any of the berries it might be interested in. . . .

"We must have carried on a one-sided conversation for about five minutes, with . . . the bear steadily grinding its teeth. Finally, it turned around and ambled back down the Trail before crashing off into the woods."

THRU-HIKER BILL IRWIN

riverbed to the road running across the top of the dam, Fontana Dam is the tallest dam in the eastern United States. Tired, sweaty hikers can take a free hot shower at the dam's visitors' center.

The Great Smoky Mountains

After crossing over the dam, the Appalachian Trail enters the Great Smoky Mountains National Park. More than 9 million visitors come to this park each year—more than visit any other U.S. national park. The Appalachian Trail through the park follows along a state boundary. Hikers along the Trail here can actually walk with one foot in Tennessee and the other foot in North Carolina!

18

The forest protected by this national park was never scraped away by glaciers. It is the most ecologically diverse forest in the United States, with more than 100 kinds of trees, about 1,500 different kinds of flowers— and 2,000 kinds of mushrooms! Some of the park is virgin forest—never been cut, never been farmed. Some of the individual trees found in the park are the largest and oldest known examples of their kind.

There are lots of animals in the park, too. White-tailed deer, rabbits, raccoons, groundhogs, and skunks are common. Lucky hikers sometimes see or hear one of the

A deer grabs an early morning snack, keeping a wary eye on the photographer.

A red wolf about to be released after being fitted with a radio collar.

200 or so rare red wolves that live in the park. They look and sound a lot like coyotes, which also roam the park. Unlike the coyotes, though, almost all of the wolves wear radio collars that have been fitted onto them by biologists studying this endangered species. About 400 to 600 black bears live in the park. Most of the bears are very shy, but a few make pests of themselves going after food carried by overnight campers.

"I glanced thirty yards below me and saw an entire herd of twelve to fourteen wild boars—from three-hundred-pound sows to cat-sized piglets—scampering through a thicket. I later learned that the boars were descendants of the Russian wild boars introduced to the area in 1910 by a lodge keeper who had imported them to serve as game for his clientele."

THRU-HIKER DAVID BRILL

David Brill, a recent college graduate, wrote a book about his Appalachian Trail thru-hike.

The boars, being imports, are not a natural part of the Smokies ecosystem. They do a lot of damage in the forest, tearing up the ground with their tusks, looking for acorns and other food.

An exposed vein of white quartz along the trail in the Great Smoky Mountains.

21

In 1540, the Spanish explorer Hernando De Soto passed through the mountains at Hot Springs, looking for gold. He didn't find any.

About midway along the Trail's path through the Great Smoky Mountains National Park comes Clingmans Dome. At 6,642 feet (2,024 meters) above sea level, Clingmans Dome is the highest point on the entire Appalachian Trail. There's an observation tower on top of this mountain, and hikers can climb it for spectacular views of the parkland all around.

The Trail continues along through the park northeast of Clingmans Dome. Here, so high up in the mountains, different kinds of trees grow. Lower on the mountainsides are mostly broad-leafed trees that lose their leaves in the wintertime, especially oaks. At higher elevations, most of the trees have evergreen needles, and the most common tree is the Fraser fir.

A few miles up the Trail from Clingmans Dome is Charlie's Bunion—5,375 feet (1,638 meters)—an unusual rock feature created by a landslide in 1929. Charlie's Bunion got its name when the two hikers who discovered it (one of them named Charlie) decided that the rocks there stuck out just like the big bunion on Charlie's toe.

Davenport Gap to the Virginia Border

The Appalachian Trail leaves the Great Smoky Mountains National Park at Davenport Gap. For the next 218 miles (351 kilometers), until it crosses over into Virginia, the Trail winds along the border between two states, which is also the border between two more national forests: Pisgah National Forest in North Carolina and Cherokee National Forest in Tennessee.

Just a few of these miles up the Trail is Max Patch, a 230-acre (93-hectare) grassy mountaintop. Max Patch used to be a family farm, and sheep and cattle grazed there only a few decades ago. In 1982 the U.S. Forest Service bought Max Patch to be part of the Appalachian Trail. They've kept it grassy and clear of trees, and at 4,629 feet (1,411 meters) above sea level it offers hikers terrific clear views of the Smokies to the south and Mount Mitchell (the highest peak in the United States east of the Mississippi River) to the east.

A few miles north of Max Patch, the Appalachian Trail runs right through the center of the old resort town of Hot Springs. During the 1800s, the mineral-rich water

Grassy Ridge, in the Roan Highlands. This is one of the many "balds" in the southern Appalachians.

that bubbles up out of the ground there made Hot Springs a fashionable health spa. At the north end of Hot Springs, the Trail crosses the French Broad River, a popular place for whitewater rafting.

Up the Trail from Hot Springs is Big Bald. "Balds" are a special feature of the southern Appalachians. These tree-less mountaintops are not treeless because of glacier action, like the barren, arctic-climate mountaintops in New England. Here, in the warmer South, the balds *may* have been first created by fires set by Native Americans many centuries ago. No one knows for sure. Grass grows on the balds, and farmers have used them for grazing cattle and sheep.

Farther up the Trail is Roan High Knob, atop Roan Mountain. At 6,285 feet (1,916 meters) above sea level, this mountain is the last place where northbound hikers will climb above 6,000 feet until the Trail reaches Mount Washington in New Hampshire. Roan Mountain may be the coldest spot along the southern part of the Appalachian Trail.

North of Roan Mountain, the Trail's up-and-downing takes hikers over several more balds before crossing over into Virginia, near Damascus.

Virginia and WEST VIRGINIA

There's more of the Appalachian Trail in Virginia—more than 500 miles (805 kilometers) of it—than in any other state. Much of the Trail in Virginia and West Virginia follows long ridgelines—strings of mountains run together with gentle dips instead of deep valleys or gaps in between.

There's less steep up-and-downing than in Georgia, North Carolina, and Tennessee, so the hiking is easier.

The Friendliest Town on the Trail

The Appalachian Trail runs right through the small town of Damascus, Virginia, just north of the Virginia/Tennessee border. Damascus is called the hiker-friendliest town on the whole Trail. Every year in May, Damascus hosts a Trail Days festival and hiker parade celebrating the Appalachian Trail.

Just north of Damascus, the Trail shares the route of the Virginia Creeper Trail for a short stretch. The Virginia

25

Creeper runs for 23 miles (37 kilometers) along an old railroad bed that winds through the mountains. It's a popular route for mountain bikers.

A little farther up the Trail is Whitetop Mountain, at 5,520 feet (1,682 meters), the second-highest peak in Virginia. The top of the highest peak, Mount Rogers, at 5,729 feet (1,746 meters), can be reached by a half-mile side trail a few miles farther along. The tiny town of Whitetop hosts an annual springtime Ramp Festival. Ramps are strong-tasting, onionlike vegetables that grow in the southern Appalachian mountains. Many hikers who camp out along the Appalachian Trail use ramps to spice up their cooking.

You may see wild ponies along the section of the Trail just beyond Mount Rogers. And you'll follow the Trail through a natural rock tunnel at Wilburn Ridge.

Wild ponies grazing in Grayson Highlands State Park, Virginia.

McAfee Knob sits on top of Catawba Mountain. Many hikers have used this sandstone outcropping to admire the incredible view.

On Sinking Creek Mountain, hikers heading north cross the Eastern Continental Divide for the last time on the Trail. (South of this point, the Trail crossed this dividing line several times, in Georgia and North Carolina.) East of the Eastern Continental Divide, all running water flows to the Atlantic Ocean. West of it, all water flows to the Mississippi River. Farther up the Trail from this point, all the way to Maine, all of the water that you see along the Trail—rain, lakes, streams, and rivers alike—eventually will make its way to the Atlantic Ocean.

The Trail passes over McAfee Knob slightly to the west of Roanoke, Virginia. Even though it's "only" 3,201 feet high (976 meters), McAfee Knob offers perhaps the best views of surrounding countryside in Virginia. Lots of day-hikers visit McAfee Knob on weekends when the weather is good.

"Several plants along the trail are tasty and healthful. One of these is the ramp. . . . I've eaten many of them, and they are good. There is wild ground lettuce and branch lettuce. . . . Both make a good salad green. . . . Young watercress, picked from spring water, is another delicacy. It will cook up or chop up readily with any of the other edible wild plants, and can be used in sandwiches. Leaves from peppermint and spearmint plants make a tea. A good method is to pick a [mint] plant, hang it on your pack to wilt and dry as you hike, then put it in a plastic bag to dry to the crumbling stage."

THRU-HIKER
CHUCK EBERSOLE

Chuck Ebersole, having recently retired from the Navy, thru-hiked the Appalachian Trail in 1964 with his son Johnny.

Down in the Great Valley (here called the Valley of Virginia), the Trail crosses Interstate 81 and heads for the Blue Ridge string of mountains, which stretches north to the Potomac River. The Blue Ridge Parkway and then Skyline Drive run near the ridgeline of the Blue Ridge through some of America's most popular parklands. So does the Appalachian Trail, close to but mostly off the road, for the next 200 or so miles.

Up the Trail a bit, half a mile north of Rt. 714, is Button Hill. There used to be a clothing factory near here, and if you look carefully you'll probably find buttons in the dirt near the Trail.

A little farther on is Apple Orchard Mountain. A side trail here—about a 3-mile (5-kilometer) round trip—leads to waterfalls. They're very exciting when the water's high after a rain. Back on the Trail, on the north side of Apple Orchard Mountain, the Trail takes you under the Guillotine—a huge boulder stuck between rocks.

Soon, the Trail crosses the James River. Way downstream, where the river empties into the Chesapeake Bay, settlers from England in 1607 started the first permanent and successful European colony in North America—Jamestown.

By now, you're nearly one-third of the way up the Trail from Georgia to Maine.

Soon the Trail crosses Crabtree Farm Road. From there, a 2-mile (3-kilometer) side trail will take you to Crabtree Falls, one of the highest waterfalls in the eastern United States.

"A rattler I saw on the trail along here [near the Blue Ridge Parkway] had 10 rattles. I know, because I counted them. He was stretched out on a log that was about waist-high off the ground. I had started to put my leg over the log but when I spotted the snake I did a rapid dance backward. I made such a wide detour around the rattler that I quite effectively lost the trail for five minutes."

THRU-HIKER
DOROTHY LAKER

Dorothy Laker thru-hiked the Appalachian Trail three times, in 1957, 1964, and 1972.

Timber rattlesnakes can be found along the Appalachian Trail in every state except Maine. They prefer dry, rocky places, and they sound their rattles when threatened. If you see one, leave it alone! Its bite probably won't kill you, but it's very painful. If you're bitten, get to a doctor as soon as possible.

This timber rattlesnake was found in Talus Field, in the Shenandoah National Park.

29

Shenandoah National Park

A couple of miles after it crosses U.S. 64 at Rockfish Gap, the Appalachian Trail enters Shenandoah National Park, the first really big national park set aside in the eastern United States. The federal government first decided that there would be a park here in 1926, but the park wasn't actually created until the mid-1930s. In creating the park, several hundred mostly impoverished families were moved to new homes outside the park.

Even though forest now once again covers almost all of the park, hikers today can still see signs along the Trail that the area was once farmed. Some of these signs are apple trees and old rock walls that used to edge cornfields. Nearly two million people visit Shenandoah National Park each year, mostly to hike the park's 500 miles (805 kilometers) of trails—including the Appalachian Trail, which runs the length of the park near Skyline Drive. (Skyline Drive mostly weaves through gaps in the mountains, while the Appalachian Trail mostly follows the mountain peaks.)

Almost everybody who spends a day along the Trail in Shenandoah National Park sees some white-tailed deer. Since they're not hunted in the park, the deer have become surprisingly tame. Other wildlife abound in the park as well, from wild turkeys to turkey buzzards, from bees to black bears.

There may even be mountain lions in Shenandoah National Park. Early settlers killed most or all of the

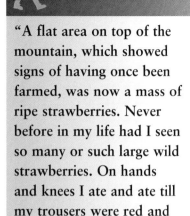

mountain lions (also called cougars) in the Appalachian Mountains, because the mountain lions killed their sheep and chickens and other livestock. Mountain lions were long thought to be extinct in these hills—but now, once in a while, people do report seeing them in the woods.

The Appalachian Trail leaves Shenandoah National Park near Front Royal. Just past where the Trail leaves the park, hikers may see some very different kinds of wildlife. The Trail there runs alongside the National Zoological Park Conservation and Research Center. No trespassing is allowed, and a sign on the fence reads "Violators Will Be Eaten."

A long day's walk later, the Trail leaves Virginia and enters West Virginia, after following along the states' border for a stretch. There are only a few miles of the Trail in West Virginia, leading to Harpers Ferry, where the Appalachian Trail Conference (ATC) has its headquarters. The ATC helps to coordinate the hundreds of volunteers who help maintain the Appalachian Trail. It also offers lots of information about the Trail at its headquarters as well as through the mail.

"A flat area on top of the mountain, which showed signs of having once been farmed, was now a mass of ripe strawberries. Never before in my life had I seen so many or such large wild strawberries. On hands and knees I ate and ate till my trousers were red and my belly was full."

THRU-HIKER
RAYMOND BAKER

Raymond Baker, a retired dairy farmer, thru-hiked the Appalachian Trail in 1964.

In 1859, a white abolitionist (anti-slavery activist) named John Brown tried to raid the U.S. arsenal at Harpers Ferry. Brown and his followers wanted to steal weapons to arm Virginia's slaves for a war against slavery. They were stopped by U.S. Army troops commanded by Colonel Robert E. Lee. John Brown was convicted of treason and hanged.

Maryland and PENNSYLVANIA

The Appalachian Trail in Maryland and Pennsylvania runs up the South Mountain ridgeline (part of the eastern ranges of the Appalachian mountains) toward Harrisburg, Pennsylvania. Near Harrisburg, the Trail crosses over the Great Valley, called the Cumberland Valley here. The Trail then climbs up into part of the western ranges of the Appalachians, the Kittatinny ridge. The Trail follows the Kittatinny ridge northeast all the way into New Jersey.

The Potomac River

The Appalachian Trail crosses over the Potomac River into Maryland just north of Harpers Ferry. There, for almost 3 miles (5 kilometers), it follows an absolutely flat path alongside the Potomac River. This is the historic Chesapeake and Ohio (C&O) Canal Towpath. The C&O Canal was built in the mid-1800s as a trade route from Washington, D.C., to Cumberland, Maryland. Today, the 185-mile (298-kilometer) towpath, once used by mules dragging boats up the canal, is a popular biking and hik-

An old lock on the C&O Canal. The towpath is between the canal and the Potomac River, which is just on the other side of the trees on the left.

ing trail. It also makes up the largest part of the Potomac Heritage National Scenic Trail.

North of the C&O Canal, the Appalachian Trail passes through a string of historically interesting state parks. In Gathland State Park is the nation's only monument to war correspondents. It honors the writers and artists who reported the Civil War. Washington Monument State Park is home to the nation's first monument to George Washington, a bottle-shaped stone structure dedicated in 1827. Just up the Trail are Greenbrier State Park and South Mountain State Park.

The Trail has come down out of the high mountains by this point. The ridgeline where the Trail runs in Mary-

The Potomac Heritage National Scenic Trail

The Potomac Heritage National Scenic Trail starts north of the Appalachian Trail, in Johnstown, Pennsylvania. It swings southwest to Ohiopyle State Park and then east to Cumberland. From there the trail follows the route of the old C&O Canal along the Potomac River to Washington, D.C. Beyond Washington, the trail follows the Potomac River south to Mount Vernon, George Washington's home. Millions of hikers, bikers, and skaters use this very popular trail each year. In the future, trail planners hope to extend the trail farther down the Potomac River, all the way to the Chesapeake Bay.

land is only about 1,000 to 2,000 feet above sea level. Outside the parkland near the Trail is farm country dotted with suburban houses. The Trail here swings through the outer reaches of the Washington/Baltimore suburbs.

A Trail marker announces where the Trail crosses the Mason-Dixon Line, the famous surveyors' line that here marks the boundary between Maryland and Pennsylvania. Two British astronomers, Charles Mason and Jeremiah Dixon, established the line in the 1760s to settle a disagreement about where the border between the colonies of Pennsylvania and Maryland really was. Later, before the Civil War, the Mason-Dixon Line marked the boundary between Southern slave states and Northern free states.

The Trail in West Virginia, Maryland, and Pennsylvania near the Maryland border passes through countryside rich in Civil War history. Part of the Trail, over South Mountain in Maryland, follows the route taken by run-

Mice are the most common campground pests along the Appalachian Trail. The usual way to mouseproof a camper's food at night is to hang it in a bag on a string. Threading a coffee-can lid or an empty tuna can on the string can help keep mice from shinning down the string for a mid-air feast.

Sometimes even these measures aren't enough. Thru-hiker Bill Irwin recalls a night in a shelter with a fellow who "had a long, rather unkempt beard and ate everything with a great deal of gusto. In the middle of one night, he started screaming, and I thought he had been attacked by a bear. Flashlights came on, everyone woke up, and he finally managed to calm down long enough to tell us what happened.

"He had eaten spaghetti for supper and gone to bed without washing his face. He awoke in the darkness to find a mouse perched on his chin, eating the spaghetti out of his mustache! He backhanded the poor mouse clear across the shelter."

THRU-HIKER BILL IRWIN

away slaves on their way to freedom in the North. Gettysburg, Pennsylvania, where more than 50,000 Civil War soldiers died in battle, is only a few miles from the Trail. Trailside markers as well as monuments in parks along the way give details of many Civil War events that took place near this part of the Trail.

The Trail heads toward Harrisburg, Pennsylvania, through Caledonia State Park, Michaux State Forest, and Pine Grove Furnace State Park. A wooden sign just north of Pine Grove Furnace marks the halfway point for Appalachian Trail thru-hikers—halfway from Georgia to

35

Maine. Beyond this point, the Trail winds through gently rolling farmland as it crosses the Cumberland Valley.

Kittatinny Ridge to the Delaware River

Near Duncannon, just west of Harrisburg, the infamous Pennsylvania rocks emerge from the Trail. Countless sharp-edged rocks pointing up from the ground make walking on the Trail a painful challenge in many places along the Kittatinny ridge, all the way to High Point, New Jersey.

The Trail crosses the Susquehanna River at Duncannon, then heads northeast through another string of parks to cross the Schuylkill River at Port Clinton. This stretch of the Trail runs through Pennsylvania Dutch country and the northwestern reaches of the greater Philadelphia area. Sections of the Trail here have been relocated many times over the years to avoid places built up for tourism or suburban housing.

Just north of Port Clinton is the Pinnacle, 1,635 feet (498 meters) above sea level, which offers a terrific view of farmland around the Trail. There are caves in the cliff just below the viewpoint.

A little farther along is Hawk Mountain Sanctuary. A visitors' center there houses displays about hawks, falcons, and eagles. As many as 20,000 of these raptors use the strong uplifting winds at Hawk Mountain to help them gain altitude during their migration south each September and October.

The Appalachian Trail crosses the Pennsylvania Turnpike's Northeast Extension at Lehigh Gap, then continues

At some points through Pennsylvania the trail becomes a jumbled ridge of rocks, requiring careful footwork.

The Western pioneer Daniel Boone was born just south of Port Clinton, Pennsylvania, in 1734. He did his first backwoods hunting and fishing and exploring in the woods around where the Trail now passes nearby. Daniel Boone and his family moved south, farther down the Appalachians, when he was about fifteen years old.

Many game birds along the Trail will flush noisily, like an explosion of feathers, from near where you're walking—wild turkey, ring-neck pheasant, quail, woodcock, grouse. Some will also try to protect their young by decoying you away from their nests, luring you away by fluttering along the ground and pretending to be wounded.

northeast around the outskirts of Allentown and Bethlehem. Through this stretch, the hills get higher, and there are real mountains ahead. The Trail crosses the Delaware River—and leaves Pennsylvania—at the Delaware Water Gap.

Hawk Mountain was purchased in 1934 by Rosalie Edge to become the world's first sanctuary for birds of prey. In the fall thousands of eagles, hawks, and ospreys can be seen. The plastic owl helps to attract the raptors to this place of safety.

New Jersey and NEW YORK

The Appalachian Trail in New Jersey and New York first continues along the Kittatinny ridge to the northwest corner of New Jersey. There the Trail turns eastward and crosses over into the Hudson Highlands. All of the hills along the Trail from the Hudson Highlands north to Maine are part of the eastern ranges of the Appalachians. The Trail follows the Hudson Highlands to Bear Mountain. It then crosses the Hudson River and heads northeast through the Taconics toward Connecticut.

Kittatinny Ridge to the Hudson Highlands

The Delaware River is wide and shallow where the Appalachian Trail crosses it at the Pennsylvania/New Jersey border. Over many years, the river has carved a steep, deep cut for itself through the Kittatinny ridge here. This spectacular cut is called the Delaware Water Gap. The area around the gap is popular with hikers and canoers

from Philadelphia, New York City, and the northern New Jersey suburbs.

The Appalachian Trail rolls northward from the Delaware Water Gap through Worthington State Forest. A few miles up the Trail is Sunfish Pond. This beautiful little lake was formed thousands of years ago by a glacier, which dug out a hole and then left behind melt water and streambeds to feed the pond when the glacier retreated. Sunfish Pond is the southernmost glacial lake or pond on the Appalachian Trail. There are many more such ponds farther north.

Sharp-eyed northbound thru-hikers in New Jersey begin to notice more and bigger rocks sticking out of the ground all around. Left behind by glaciers, these rocks are a preview of things to come in Connecticut and points north in New England, where there are rocks and boulders everywhere.

The Trail continues along the ridgeline beside the Delaware River all the way north to High Point, in the northwest corner of New Jersey. There's a short side trail leading to High Point monument—the highest spot in New Jersey.

After High Point, the Trail turns northeast and runs near the border between New Jersey and New York. It passes through Wawayanda State Park and Hewitt State Forest, and then crosses over into the state of New York. The mountains along this stretch of Trail are known as the Hudson Highlands.

Prospect Rock, 1,433 feet (437 meters) above sea level, the first landmark on the Trail in New York, is also the highest point on the Trail in New York. There's a great view from Prospect Rock of Greenwood Lake to the east. But it's not all downhill from here—there's a lot of up-and-downing ahead.

Sterling Forest to the Taconics

The Trail soon passes through a section of Sterling Forest. This 20,000-acre (8,000-hectare) forest has long been the largest privately owned chunk of undeveloped land so close to New York City. Real estate developers, nature preservation groups, and politicians have fought for years over whether this land should be left wild or have houses built on it. In 1996, Congress and the states of New York

41

and New Jersey finally bought most of Sterling Forest near the Appalachian Trail, intending to keep it in its natural condition for years to come.

From Sterling Forest, the Trail heads toward Bear Mountain. This was the very first section of the Appalachian Trail to be completed, in 1923. It's also the section of the Trail closest to New York City, and you can catch glimpses of the New York skyline from viewpoints along or near the Trail in the park. The high point of the

A view of the Hudson River from Bear Mountain State Park.

Trail here is Bear Mountain itself, 1,305 feet (398 meters) above sea level.

There's a zoo on Bear Mountain that holds many animals native to the area around the Trail in New York, including black bears. (There's also a famous statue here of another native of the area—the poet Walt Whitman.) A short stretch of the Trail inside the zoo passes underground. At only 124 feet (38 meters) above sea level, this is the lowest point on the entire Appalachian Trail.

The Trail crosses the Hudson River at Bear Mountain Bridge, which offers terrific views up and down the wide, deep river. Just beyond the bridge, the Trail passes over a mountaintop called Anthony's Nose, named after General "Mad Anthony" Wayne, a local Revolutionary War hero. You're on National Guard training grounds here, and you may see soldiers practicing military maneuvers. Hikers are warned to stay on the Trail.

From here, the Appalachian Trail cuts across New York suburbs, through several parks and towns. The hills here are called the Taconics. There's an Appalachian Trail train station in this stretch, with weekend trains taking hikers to and from New York City's Grand Central Station. Here, too, is found what's thought to be the largest oak tree along the Trail—the Dover Oak, measuring more than 19 feet (6 meters) around and estimated to be 300 years old.

"Following the ridge paralleling Greenwood Lake, I ran into two young raccoons crossing over the bare rocks. They paid no attention to me until I scared one up a tree. Not the best climber in the world, the raccoon only went high enough to be out of reach. There he stopped and peeked around the trunk at me."

THRU-HIKER
RAYMOND BAKER

43

Connecticut and MASSACHUSETTS

The Appalachian Trail cuts across the northwestern corner of Connecticut, through the hills near the beautiful Housatonic River, heading northward to Massachusetts. In Massachusetts, the Trail runs straight up the Berkshires to Vermont.

The Housatonic River Valley

Just beyond Pawling, New York, the Trail crosses over into northwestern Connecticut, heading toward the Housatonic River valley. The countryside here is more hilly than mountainous, although some of the walking is quite steep. There are lots of little streams and an astonishing number and variety of rocks—from little loose stones on the Trail to whole walls of rock rising up out of the earth, with plenty of mid-sized boulders in between—all left behind by glaciers.

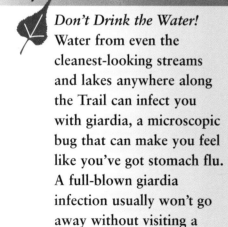

Don't Drink the Water! **Water from even the cleanest-looking streams and lakes anywhere along the Trail can infect you with giardia, a microscopic bug that can make you feel like you've got stomach flu. A full-blown giardia infection usually won't go away without visiting a doctor for special medicine.**

Along the Trail in Connecticut, you can see many traces of the farmers who long ago cleared the land nearby. The trees have grown up here over the past century, where once there were cow pastures and cornfields. But some of the farmers' old stone walls remain. Some of the farmers' homes remain, too—classic New England farmhouses lovingly preserved in and around quaint villages that now house and serve more weekending New Yorkers than working farmers.

The Appalachian Trail in Connecticut curves north along and near the scenic Housatonic River. It also crosses U.S. 7, a mostly two-lane country highway that runs all the way from southern Connecticut to Montreal, Canada. The Trail stays near U.S. 7 clear through Massachusetts and well into Vermont.

> "I hike for no immediate reason. It's the person I *become* when I hike that drives me to continue."
>
> THRU-HIKER
> CINDY ROSS

Wild turkeys were once so numerous, and so valued for their delicious meat, that Benjamin Franklin thought they should be the U.S. national bird. (The other Founding Fathers disagreed and named the bald eagle instead.) Turkeys were hunted so much that only about 30,000 were left in the United States in 1930. Today, biologists estimate, there are 4.3 million of them. Many live in the woods along the Appalachian Trail.

Skunks, being well-armed with their smelly spray, aren't much afraid of hikers. They are most active at night, and they are common campground pests all along the Trail. Sometimes they even make their homes in trail shelters!

Thru-hikers need to eat a lot of food to keep going, and wild berries are a favorite Trail treat. Hikers heading north through the spring and summer find first strawberries, then blueberries, then raspberries and blackberries coming ripe and ready to be eaten. Since berries down in a valley ripen sooner than berries high up on a mountain, and berries down south ripen before those growing farther north, thru-hikers heading north while going up and down the mountains can find ripe, fresh berries over a delightfully long season.

The Berkshires

Just before leaving Connecticut, at Sages Ravine, the Trail climbs yet another Bear Mountain, this one the highest peak—2,316 feet (706 meters)—in Connecticut. Here the Trail is heading into a string of mountains called the Berkshires. The Trail follows the Berkshires north all the way through western Massachusetts—a 90-mile (145-kilometer) rollercoaster.

The second-highest hill on this Massachusetts rollercoaster comes not far up the Trail from Sages Ravine—Mount Everett, 2,602 feet (793 meters) above sea level. The Trail then drops to cross U.S. 7 and the Housatonic River once again.

The Berkshires are a popular "get away from it all" destination for city folks living in Boston, New York, and points in between. There are arts festivals in the summer, skiing in the winter, and many hiking trails to explore. The Appalachian Trail connects with many of these side trails as it works its way north through the mountains.

The Trail passes through several towns in Massachusetts, including Cheshire, best known as the home of the "Big Cheese." Local supporters of President Thomas Jefferson gave him an enormous block of cheese, which he put on display at the White House. There's a monument to the Big Cheese right on the Trail, just across from the post office in Cheshire.

Just up the Trail from Cheshire is Mount Greylock, at 3,491 feet (1,064 meters) the highest mountain in Massachusetts, and the first mountaintop above 3,000 feet the northbound Trail has crossed since Virginia. You can climb the stone tower (a war memorial) at the top of the mountain for great views of not only the Berkshires but also the Catskills and Taconic mountains in nearby New York, and the Green Mountains in Vermont—which are just a little farther ahead on the Appalachian Trail.

The writer Herman Melville could see Mount Greylock out the window from his desk. In the wintertime, the mountain looked to him like a great white whale—and a great white whale became the star of his greatest novel, *Moby Dick*.

For some hikers this sign points the way over the next hill. For others, it points the way to Mount Katahdin.

Vermont and NEW HAMPSHIRE

The Appalachian Trail in Vermont runs north through the Green Mountains, then turns eastward at Killington and heads for New Hampshire. In New Hampshire, the Trail cuts northeast, up and over the White Mountains, including the mighty Presidential Range.

Vermont, the Green Mountain State

At the Massachusetts/Vermont border, the Appalachian Trail joins the Long Trail. The 269-mile (433-kilometer) Long Trail, completed in 1931, runs from the Massachusetts border north to the Canadian border.

For 104 miles (167 kilometers), the Appalachian Trail follows the same route as the Long Trail in Vermont, mostly through Green Mountain National Forest. These are serious mountains here, many of them very popular for skiing in the winter.

Several generations ago, farmers cut down most of the trees in Vermont. The poor, stony soil and steep hills made for hard farming. Most of the state's farmland has long since been abandoned. Over most of Vermont, the woods have regrown, with more pine trees and other conifers than are seen farther south. You can still see stone walls and the ruins of farmhouses built by long-gone farmers in the woods along and near the Trail here.

There's a fire tower on top of Glastonbury Mountain—3,748 feet (1,142 meters)—that offers spectacular views of Mount Greylock and the Berkshires to the south, the Green Mountains all around, and the Trail up ahead.

Farther up the trail is Stratton Mountain. Trail lore has it that on top of Stratton Mountain, checking out the view in a tall tree, Benton MacKaye first had the idea for a trail running along the peaks of the Appalachians from Georgia to Maine. In time, MacKaye's idea became the Appalachian Trail.

The Trail crosses Clarendon Gorge on a suspension bridge high above the water below. Hot-weather hikers often prefer to walk down into the gorge instead of over the bridge, so they can take a dip in the swimming hole there.

A few miles north is Killington Peak, at 4,235 feet (1,291 meters) above sea level, the highest point on or near the Trail in Vermont. From the top of Killington, reached by a very short but steep side trail, you can see all the way from the Adirondack Mountains in New York to the west, to the White Mountains in New Hampshire to the east.

The Appalachian Trail turns eastward, toward those White Mountains, just after coming down from Killington Peak. There's a famous lodge at the foot of Killington, the Inn at Long Trail, that caters to hikers and skiers. Just

> "The woods are lovely, dark and deep. But I have promises to keep, And miles to go before I sleep."
>
> VERMONT FARMER
> AND POET
> ROBERT FROST

49

Porcupines are common campsite pests in the New England states. They aren't much afraid of anything, since they're well-protected by their sharp, barbed quills. They crave salt and are fond of gnawing on anything sweaty hikers have touched—backpacks, boots, even the toilet seats at outhouses!

past the lodge, at Maine Junction, the Long Trail continues on north to Canada. The Appalachian Trail heads east, continuing its path up the eastern ranges of the Appalachians.

The next major landmark along the Trail is Kent Pond, a glacial lake with a hiking and skiing resort on its shore. By this point, the Trail has left the Green Mountain National Forest. From here to New Hampshire the landscape is mostly hilly rather than mountainous, with many beautiful lakes. In the flatter, wetter parts of the Trail, hikers find a lot of mud, especially in the spring.

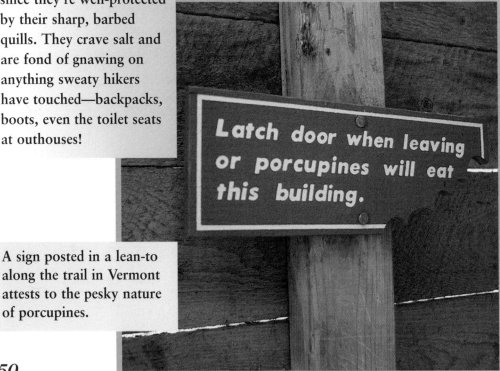

A sign posted in a lean-to along the trail in Vermont attests to the pesky nature of porcupines.

50

When the Trail crosses the Connecticut River, it also crosses the Vermont/New Hampshire border. Just over the border, the Trail goes right through the little town of Hanover, New Hampshire, home of Dartmouth College.

Beyond Hanover the hills get bigger. Smarts Mountain is 3,240 feet (987 meters) above sea level, and Mount Cube 2,911 feet (887 meters). Some of the most awesome mountains on the entire Appalachian Trail lie just ahead—the White Mountains, including the spectacular Presidentials.

"Pulling a granola bar from my pack, I sat on a rock, but no sooner had I peeled off the wrapper than a gray Canada jay landed squarely on my shoulder. . . . Soon the jay roosted on my finger and nibbled from my hand."

THRU-HIKER
DAVID BRILL

These funny, friendly birds, also called scavenger jays or camp jays, often visit hikers in the woods of Vermont, New Hampshire, and Maine, begging for food.

A Canada jay looking for another hiker willing to share a snack.

White Mountain National Forest

Just a few miles into White Mountain National Forest, Mount Moosilauke is the first mountaintop above treeline (also called timberline) that northbound hikers come across on the Appalachian Trail. In northern parts of the United States, the weather high up in the mountains is so cold and so harsh that trees can't grow there, just as trees can't grow in the Arctic. Walking up one of these mountains, you first see broad-leafed hardwood trees, such as oak and white birch, gradually giving way to more and more conifers, from pine and balsam to spruce. Finally, near the top, not even stunted, twisted spruce trees can survive. In the highest and harshest alpine (mountaintop) conditions, only lichens, little clumps of grass, and other small plants can live.

The treeline occurs at different heights on different mountains, depending on the unique conditions at each mountain. Many of the plants that grow above treeline are found only there. With no trees to block the view, unusual plantlife all around, and such weird weather conditions as occasional snow even in July and August, these mountaintops are strange and exciting places to visit.

The Appalachian Trail runs for miles at a time above treeline in the White Mountains. The most famous section of the Trail here runs through the Presidential Range, with about 25 miles (40 kilometers) of ridgewalking, most of it above treeline. There are mountains here named for five early U.S. presidents: Mount Madison, 5,363 feet (1,635 meters) above sea level; Mount Monroe, 5,385 feet

"The five-mile drag up [Mount] Moosilauke took more than three hours, bringing me for the first time above true timberline. The trees got shorter and shorter until they were only scattered clumps the size of bushes. The summit was almost nothing but acres of rocks. . . . This is a world of silence. Even a strong wind makes little noise" when not blocked by trees.

THRU-HIKER EARL SHAFFER

"It was overcast, and when I heard thunder I stopped to see what would develop. After a few minutes the thunder was behind me. I figured the storm had passed and set off again, although I felt slightly uneasy. A little later my skin began to tingle all over. As I neared the summit of Lafayette there was a crash. The storm was overhead and I was on top of a 5,200-foot [1,585-meter] mountain! I decided to lie down in order to present less of a target. I stopped for about 10 minutes until the storm passed."

THRU-HIKER BILL O'BRIEN

(1,641 meters); Mount Jefferson, 5,715 feet (1,742 meters); Mount Adams, 5,798 feet (1,767 meters); and the highest and mightiest of them all, Mount Washington, 6,288 feet (1,917 meters).

Mount Washington is a very popular tourist destination, and it can be reached by road as well as by an unusual, very steep cog railway. At the summit, there was once a large hotel, which burned to the ground in 1908. But don't be misled by all this civilization. Mount Washington is a fierce and dangerous place, with unpredictable and deadly weather possible anytime. More than 100 hikers have died after becoming stranded in unexpected snowstorms on or near Mount Washington—most of them in the summer months.

The snow-covered peak of Mount Washington is visible in the distance from this point on the trail.

54

Snow is possible every month of the year on Mount Washington—even in July and August. As for the winter weather here: The average winter daytime high temperature is only 15 degrees, and the winds are almost unbelievable. On April 12, 1934, the still-unbeaten world record for on-land wind speed was set on Mount Washington. A scientist on top of the mountain measured the wind at 231 miles per hour—and then the measuring device broke!

Beyond the Presidential Range, the Appalachian Trail heads northeast into its final state: Maine.

"The scenario is often the same: fog materializes from nowhere or a sudden snowy whiteout descends, and visibility vanishes in minutes. Hikers clad in shorts and T-shirts, who might have been basking in warm sunlight only minutes earlier, suddenly find themselves drenched, shrouded in fog or snow, and buffeted by fifty- or sixty-mile-per-hour winds—the perfect recipe for hypothermia [dangerously low body temperature]. Soon their body temperatures plunge below critical levels, their mental faculties dim, and they lie down in the snow and yield to death."

THRU-HIKER
DAVID BRILL

MAINE

The Appalachian Trail in Maine has something for every kind of nature lover—mountains, lakes, bogs, and a long stretch of wilderness far from any towns. The Trail's end point in Maine is Mount Katahdin, the most awesome mountain on the Trail.

The Home Stretch to Katahdin

Just past the New Hampshire/Maine border the Appalachian Trail passes through Mahoosuc Notch—a mile-long field of boulders that hikers must scramble around, over, and under. Even in summertime, ice can be found in pockets and cracks around these boulders. Many hikers find this is the toughest mile on the whole Appalachian Trail.

The Trail in Maine goes up and down fearsome mountains much like the Whites in New Hampshire. Ten of them higher than 2,900 feet (884 meters)—some high-

> "This famous notch, which might have been called Nightmare Valley, was a channel between steep walls, jammed with giant boulders tossed one upon the other. There were spaces between and under the boulders. Moss grew over everything. Trees were growing wherever they could find enough soil and their roots were of great help in getting over the boulders. . . . The water that flowed beneath the rocks was very cold, and frigid air welled up along the trail from the ice and icy water below. More often than not the trail went under and over the boulders, rather than around them. Spaces beneath the boulders were cramped and usually either muddy or dusty. It was not possible to wear a pack and still get through some of the tunnels under the boulders. It was a very strenuous trail, time-consuming, dangerous, and hard on gear and the seat of the pants. . . . I had a horrible time, absolutely awful. At one point I lay down on the rocks and cried." THRU-HIKER
> DOROTHY LAKER

er than 4,000 feet (1,219 meters)—are found just in the first hundred or so miles up to and including Bigelow Preserve, a 33,000-acre (13,354-hectare) state wilderness preserve. From some of these peaks you can see Mount Katahdin off in the distance.

Northeast of Bigelow Preserve, the Trail passes through some wet, boggy sections on log walkways. The "bog logs" are there not only to help hikers but also to protect the bog's fragile ecosystem from being damaged by the Trail's foot traffic.

The Appalachian Trail through Mahoosuc Notch

Maine's bogs are home to lots of wildlife—water birds, fish, moose, deer, bears, raccoons, weasels, otters, fishers, martens, and mink. There are plenty of mosquitoes and black flies, too—so be sure to bring along insect repellent!

Farther along, about halfway up the Maine section of the Appalachian Trail, the Trail crosses the Kennebec River. A free ferry service takes hikers across this wide river in the summer months. A hydroelectric plant upstream from the Trail releases lots of water at unpredictable times, raising the water level in the river suddenly and sharply. The hydroelectric plant and the river's strong current make crossing the river on foot dangerous.

Beyond the Kennebec River, just after crossing Rt. 15, the Trail enters its famous "100-mile wilderness"—a long stretch of remote, wooded trail far from any towns. There's a little bit of everything along the Trail here—mountains, lakes, ponds, streams, and some more bog walking. Most of the trees are white pines. Moose and other wildlife abound.

Henry David Thoreau, writing about Maine in the mid-1800s, said "What is most striking in the Maine wilderness is the continuousness of the forest, with fewer open intervals or glades than you had imagined. . . . It is even more grim and wild than you had anticipated, a damp and intricate wilderness. . . . Here prevail no forest laws but those of nature." Even in Thoreau's time, huge amounts of lumber were being cut and taken out of the Maine woods. But the woods were so vast and thickly

A bull moose in Baxter State Park. No photograph can show how unbelievably large these animals look when seen in person.

treed that the lumberjacks seemed to be only nibbling around the edges of the forest, with most of the forest remaining wild and untouched.

At the northern end of the quiet, isolated "100-mile wilderness" is Baxter State Park. Baxter is the largest pure wilderness preserve in the United States east of the Mississippi River. Its crowning glory is Mount Katahdin—the northern endpoint of the Appalachian Trail.

Unlike the Presidentials, Mount Katahdin stands alone, rising up from the surrounding lake-filled woods to a majestic 5,267 feet (1,605 meters) above sea level. The Trail up Mount Katahdin climbs a heart-pounding 4,000 feet (1,219 meters) in only 5 miles (8 kilometers) of hiking.

Native Americans living near Mount Katahdin said its summit was the home of Pamola, a spirit who destroyed persons who dared to climb up the mountain and approach its home. The first person known for sure to have climbed Katahdin and lived to tell about it was Charles Turner Jr., in 1804.

Near the summit of Mount Katahdin is a wide, flat plateau called the Tableland. Thoreau Spring on the Tableland is named after the nature writer Henry David Thoreau, who explored the Maine woods in 1846. Bad weather stopped him from reaching the top of Katahdin, but he's forever linked to the mountain by the report he wrote about his adventures in *The Maine Woods*:

"On the 31st of August, 1846, I left Concord in Massachusetts for Bangor and the backwoods of Maine. . . . I proposed to make excursions to Mount Ktaadn. . . .

Very few, even among backwoodsmen and hunters, have ever climbed it, and it will be a long time before the tide of fashionable travel sets that way."
Henry David Thoreau, *The Maine Woods*

Since Thoreau's time, thousands of hikers have climbed Mount Katahdin. Millions have climbed one or more of the many other mountains along the Trail. If you "seek fellowship with the wilderness," as the sign on Springer Mountain says, you, too, can find it along the Appalachian Trail.

The glacier-carved, lichen-covered toprock of the granite monolith that is the final destination for hikers of the Appalachian Trail, Mount Katahdin.

61

The Appalachian Trail is managed and maintained by the Appalachian Trail Conference, in cooperation with the federal government, various state and local parks, and thousands of volunteers working all along the Trail. If you want to help keep the Trail in good shape—or if you just want to know more about it—get in touch with the Appalachian Trail Conference, P.O. Box 807, Harpers Ferry, West Virginia 25425.

The hikers' quotes in *Step By Step Along the Appalachian Trail* were found in these books:

Brill, David. *As Far as the Eye Can See: Reflections of an Appalachian Trail Hiker.* Nashville, Tennessee: Rutledge Hill Press, 1990.

Browne, Robert A. *The Appalachian Trail: History, Humanity, and Ecology.* Stafford, Virginia: Northwoods Press, 1980.

From Katahdin to Springer Mountain: The Best Stories of Hiking the Appalachian Trail. Emmaus, Pennsylvania: Rodale Press, 1977.

Irwin, Bill, with David McCasland. *Blind Courage.* Waco, Texas: WRS Publishing, 1992.

Ross, Cindy. *A Woman's Journey on the Appalachian Trail.* Charlotte, North Carolina: East Woods Press, 1982.

Shaffer, Earl V. *Walking With Spring: The First Thru-Hike of the Appalachian Trail.* Harpers Ferry, West Virginia: Appalachian Trail Conference, 1983.

Thoreau, Henry David. *The Maine Woods: Ktaadn.* New York: Library of America, 1985.

INDEX

Page numbers in *italics* refer to illustrations.